This Messy Entertainment book belongs to:

....

....

Oscar the sea turtle

Published By Messy Entertainment Ltd 2017
ISBN 978-1-9998015-5-7
Messy Entertainment Ltd
www.messyentertainment.com

Oscar the sea turtle 2017 © Messy Entertainment Ltd
All rights reserved.

This book or any portion thereof may not be reproduced or used
in any manner whatsoever without the express written permission
of the publisher except for the use of brief quotations in a book review.

On a starry night when the moon was bright two sea turtles appeared out of the sea.

They pulled themselves up onto the beach to lay their eggs in the warm sand.

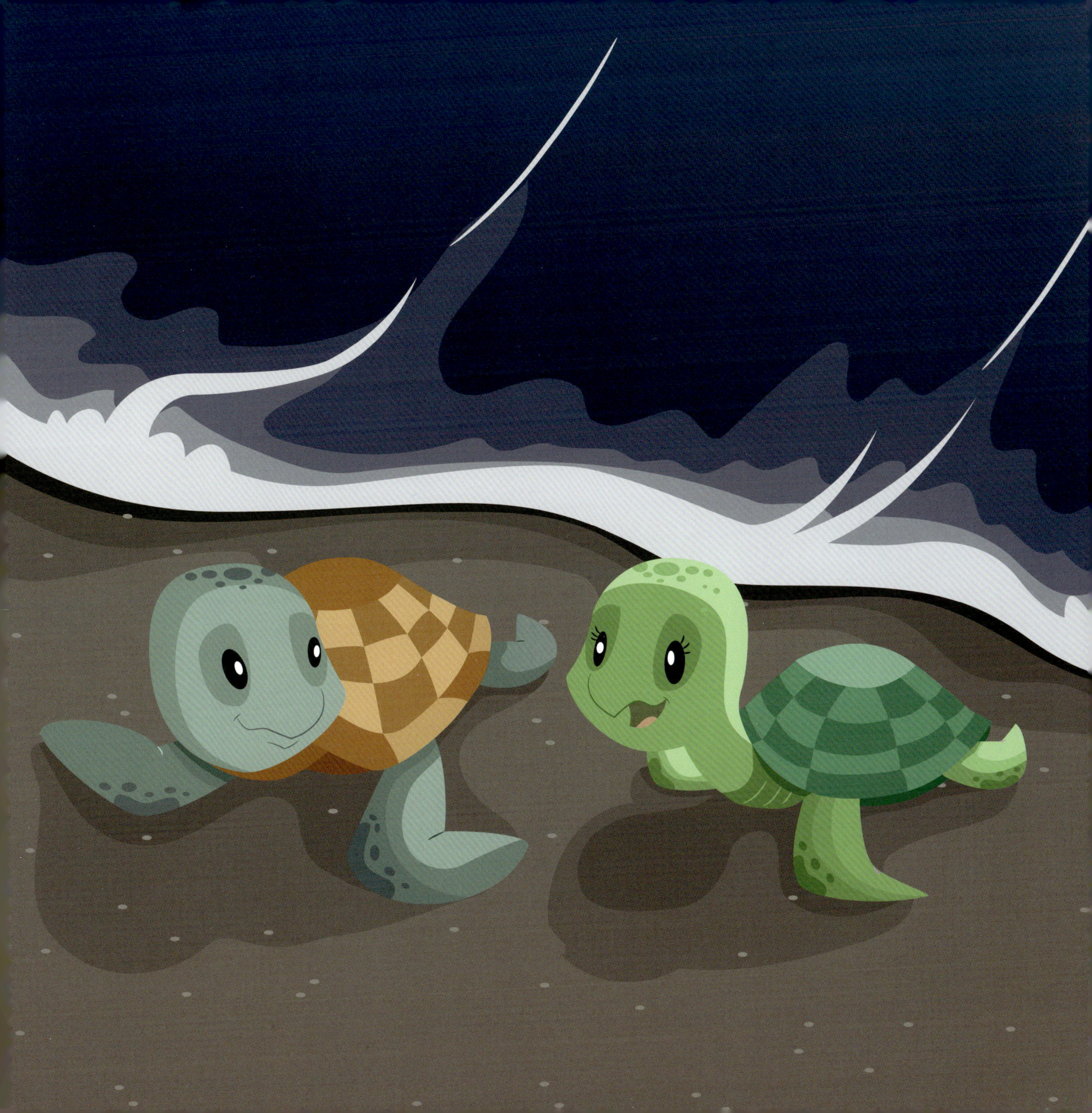

While one turtle was digging a nest she heard "I want to have two sons and I want to call them Oscar and Percy. I think I will be a good daddy".

After the eggs were wrapped up safe in their nest, mummy sea turtle looked around and smiled.

As they crawled back into the sea she said "I can't wait to meet the babies, I hope they make the long journey home safely".

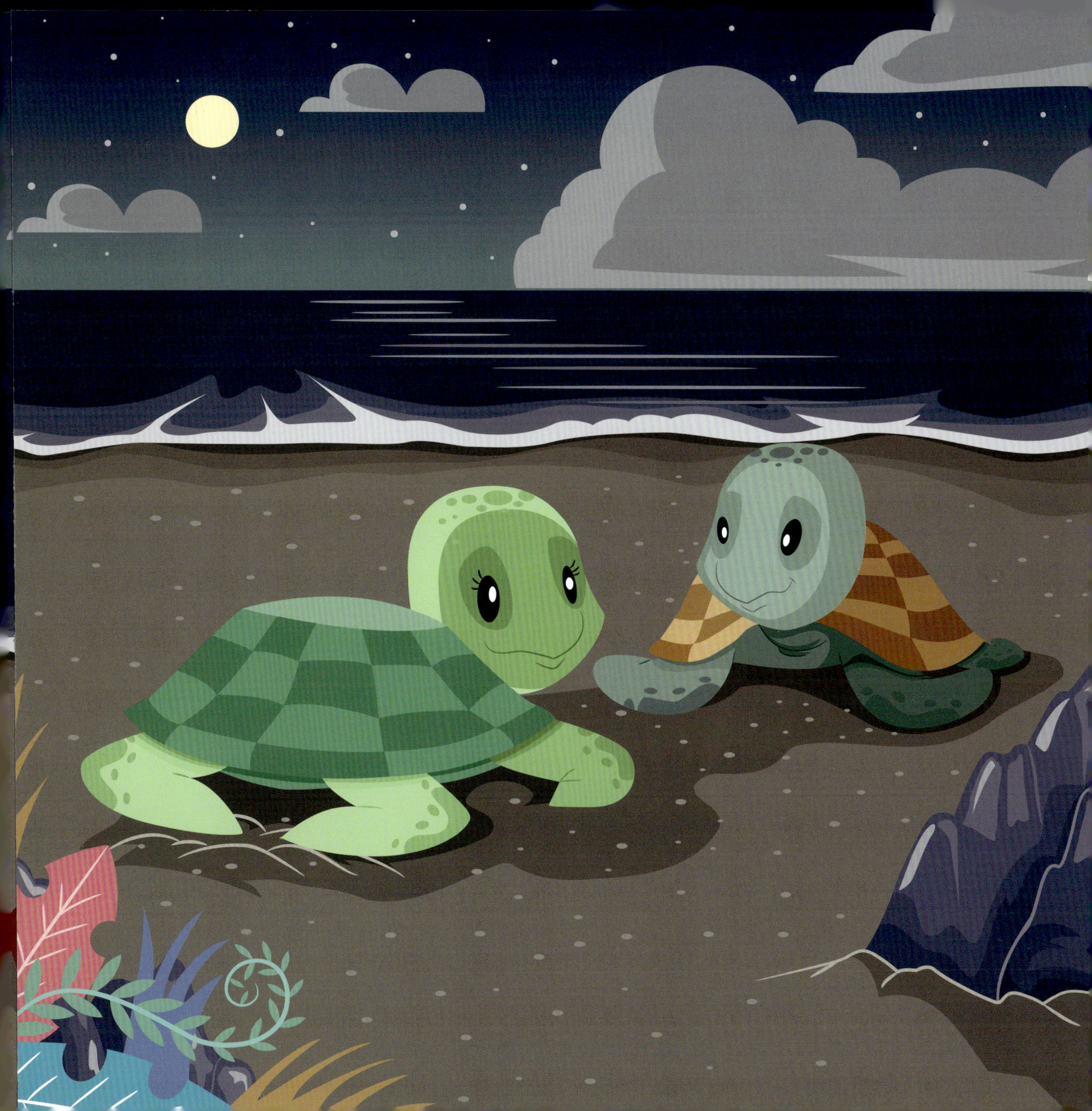

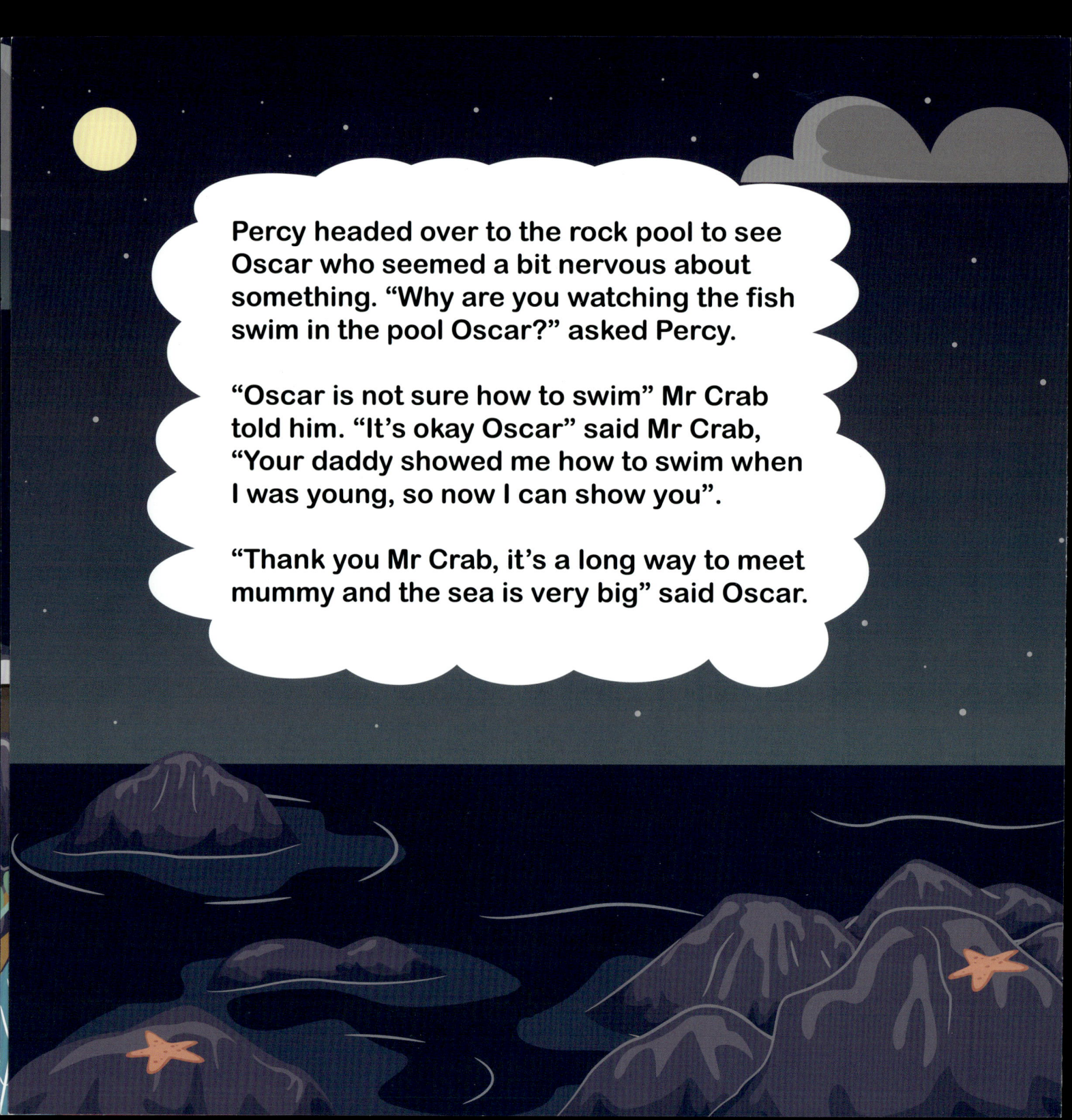

Percy headed over to the rock pool to see Oscar who seemed a bit nervous about something. "Why are you watching the fish swim in the pool Oscar?" asked Percy.

"Oscar is not sure how to swim" Mr Crab told him. "It's okay Oscar" said Mr Crab, "Your daddy showed me how to swim when I was young, so now I can show you".

"Thank you Mr Crab, it's a long way to meet mummy and the sea is very big" said Oscar.

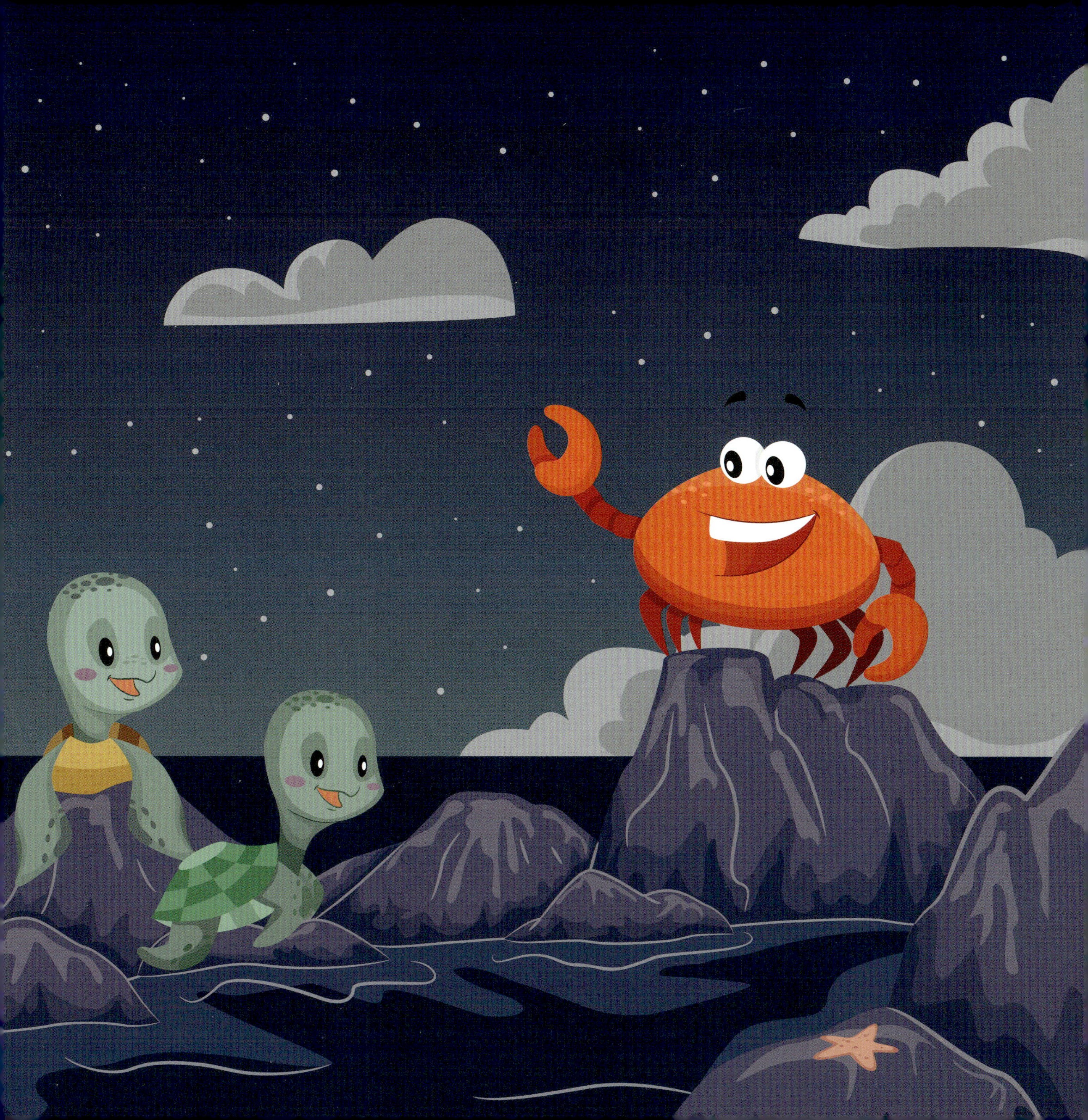

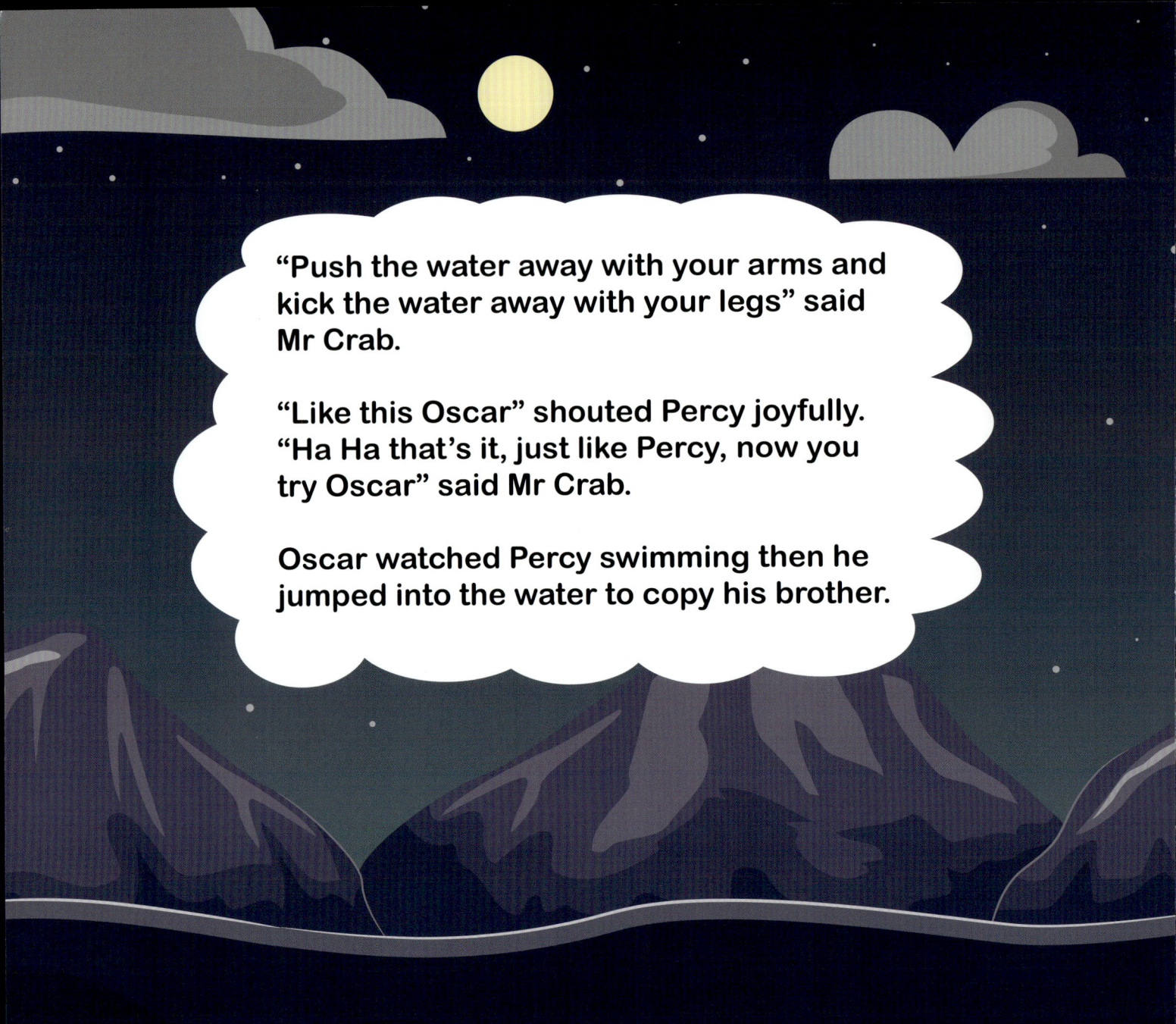

"Push the water away with your arms and kick the water away with your legs" said Mr Crab.

"Like this Oscar" shouted Percy joyfully. "Ha Ha that's it, just like Percy, now you try Oscar" said Mr Crab.

Oscar watched Percy swimming then he jumped into the water to copy his brother.

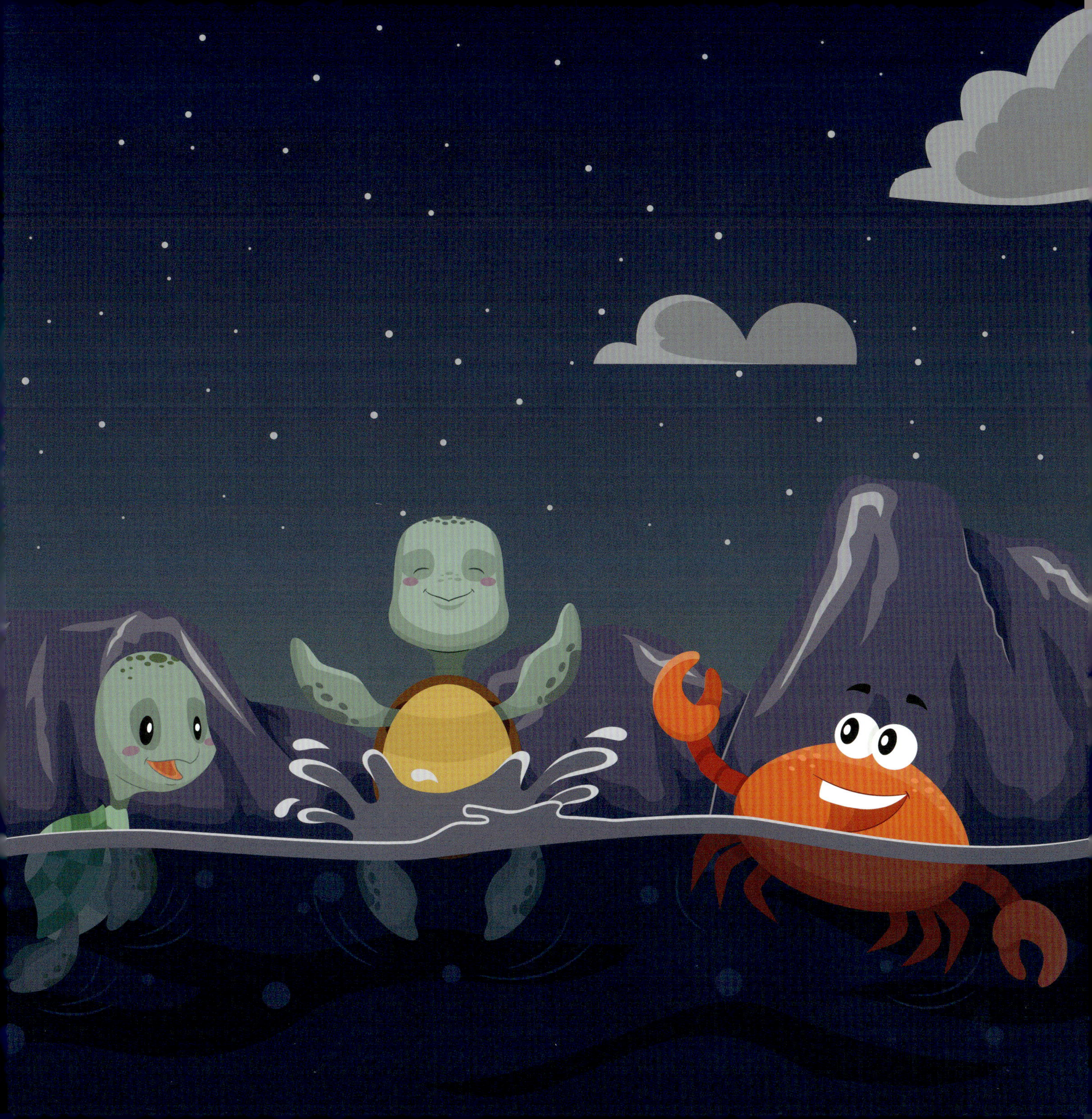

Oscar was already good at swimming but he felt nervous looking at the big open sea.

The sun started to rise, Mr Crab said to Oscar and Percy "You must go now and look for your mummy, the hungry birds will be out soon looking for breakfast".

"Goodbye Mr Crab" yelled Percy and Oscar as they headed towards the sea.

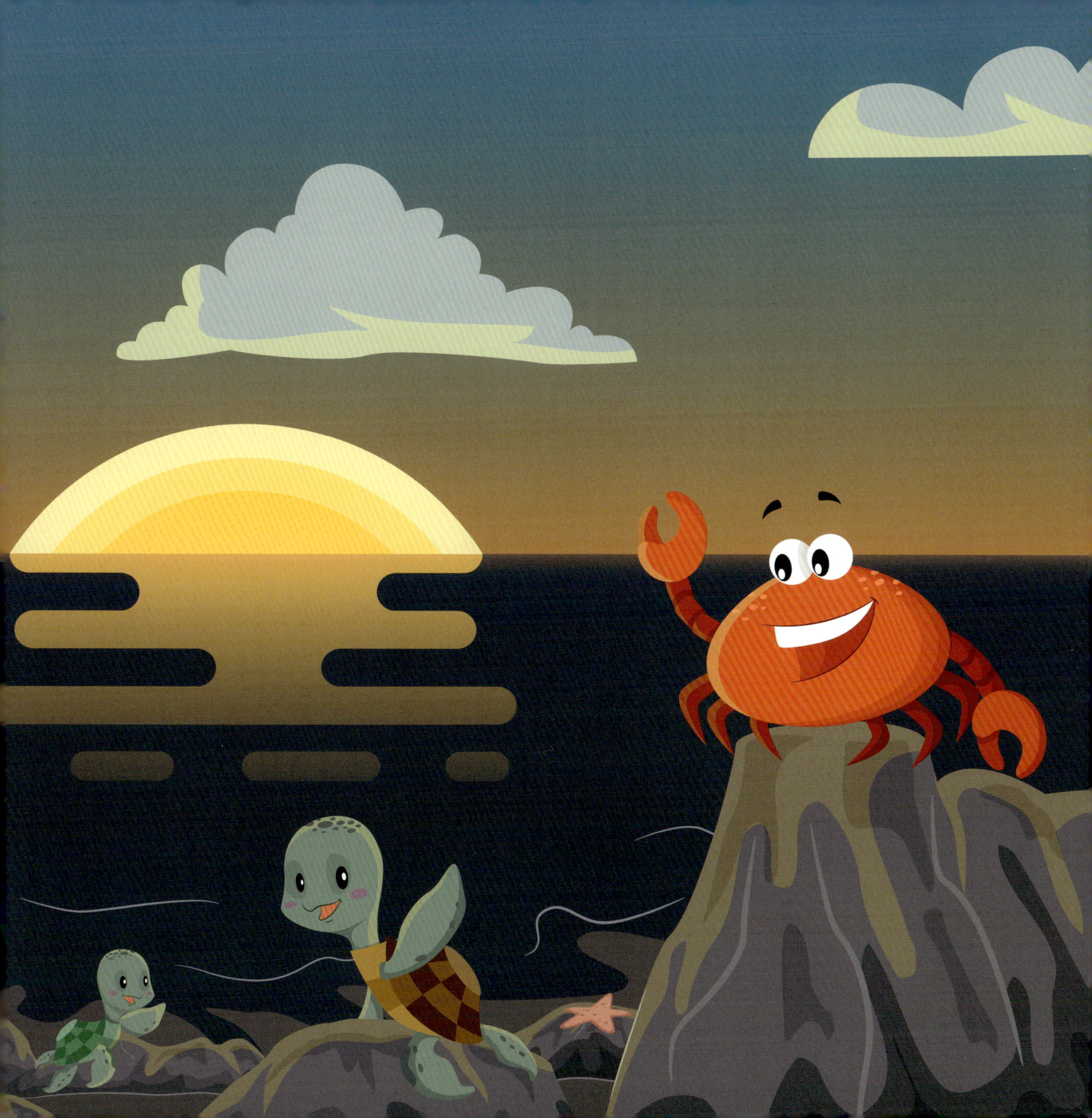

The sea was so big Oscar and Percy were not sure which way to go.

As a wise old whale came swimming by he told Oscar "I saw your mum and dad swim by here 50 days ago".

"Can you show us which way to go please?" Oscar asked.

"You must follow the shore current all the way to the reef. Do not go into the dark water or you could get into danger" explained the whale.

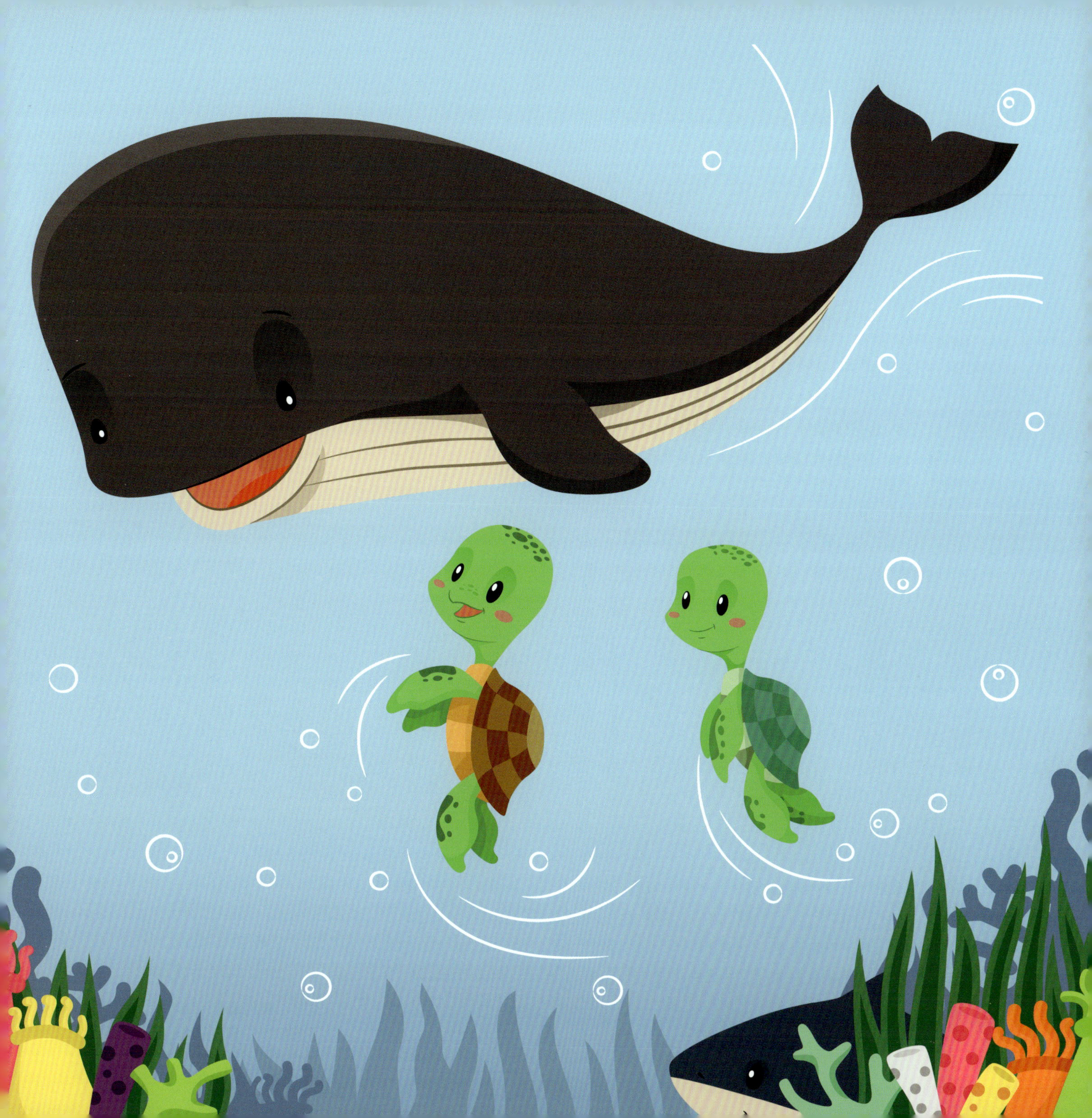

Oscar and Percy swam into the shore current and were amazed to see all the other turtles heading for the reef.

"Thank you" yelled Percy as they were whisked away by the fast moving current.

"Woo Hoo, this is fun! I can't wait to tell mummy about this" shouted Oscar joyfully.

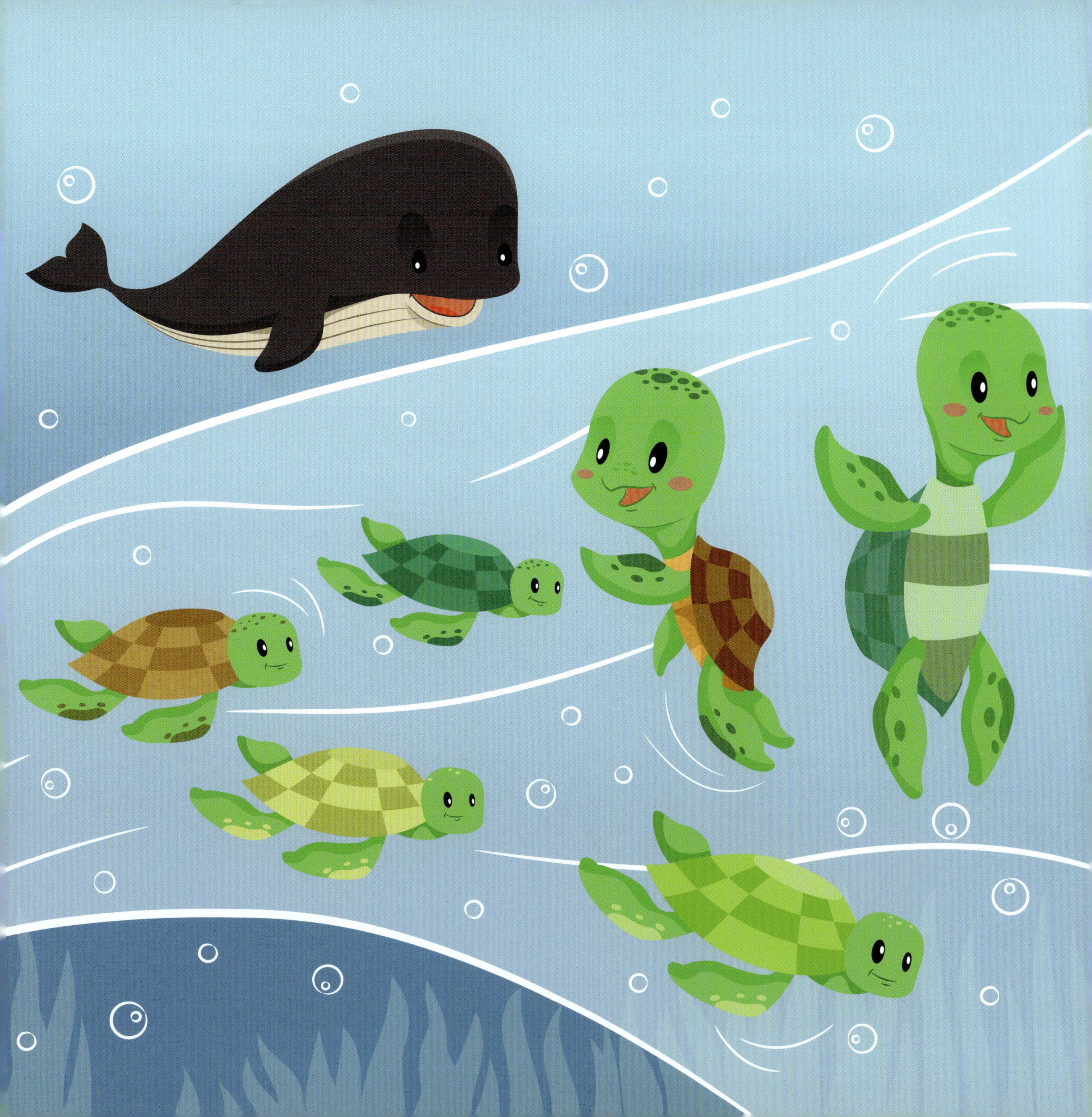

After travelling for a very long time, the water began to get shallower and the current started to slow down, Oscar was very excited to meet his parents.

They could see lots of the other sea turtles playing by the reef.

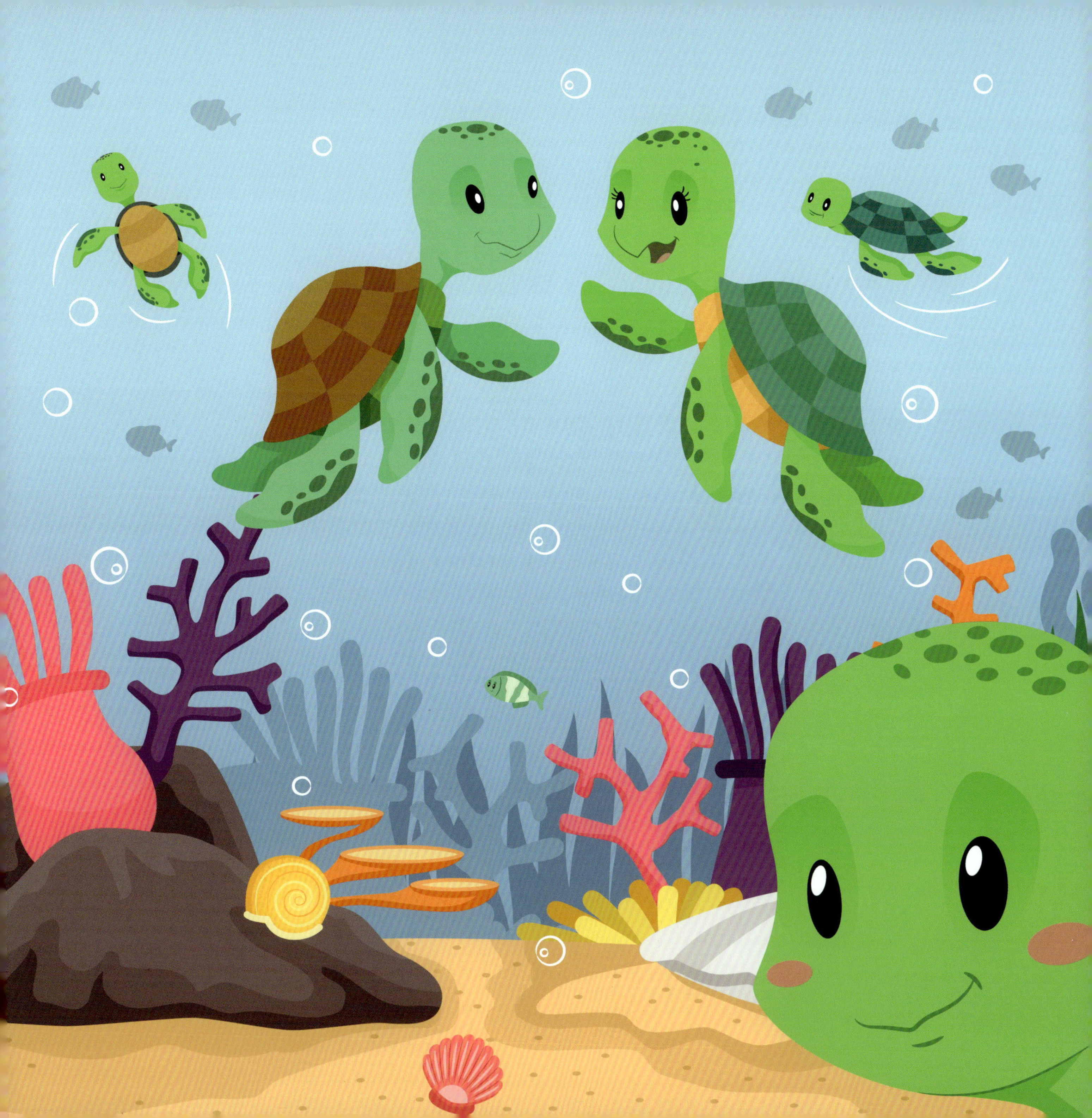

"Mum!" shouted Oscar, "Percy over here I can see mummy" Oscar yelled.

They rushed over to see their mummy with all their family. After lots of cuddles Oscar and Percy told them everything about their long journey.

Daddy sea turtle was very proud, the friends they had made helped Oscar and Percy find their way safely to the reef.

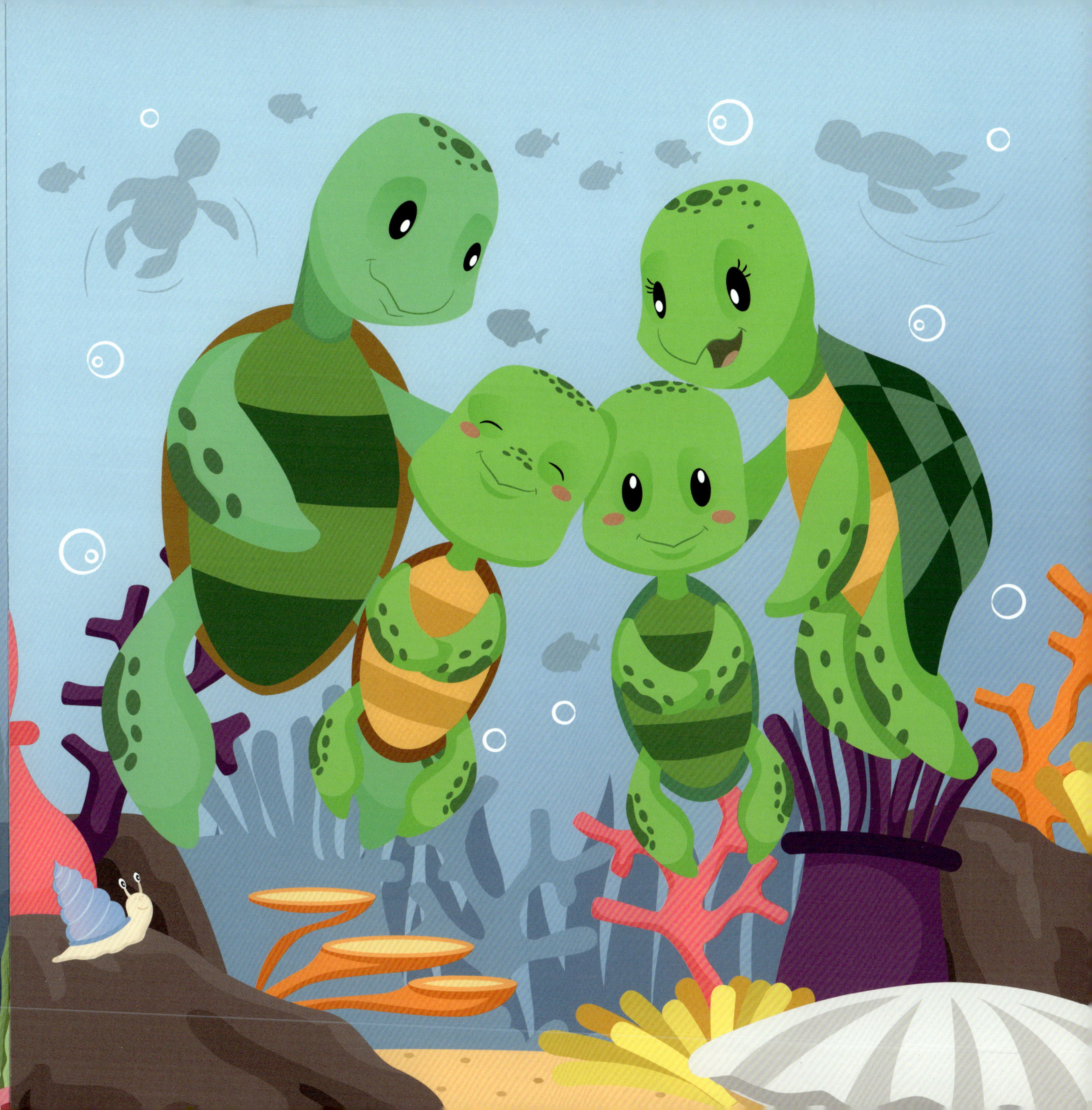

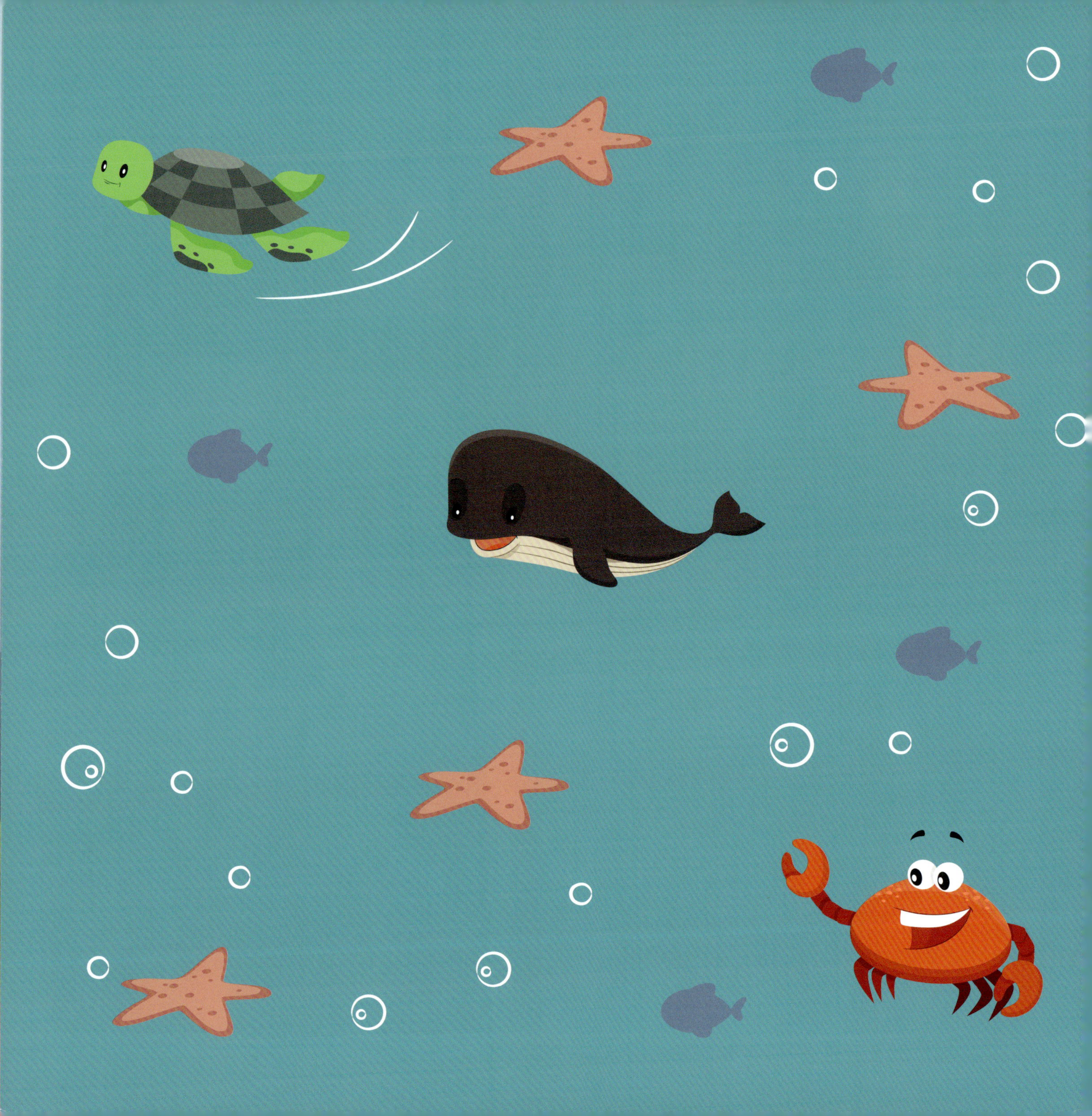

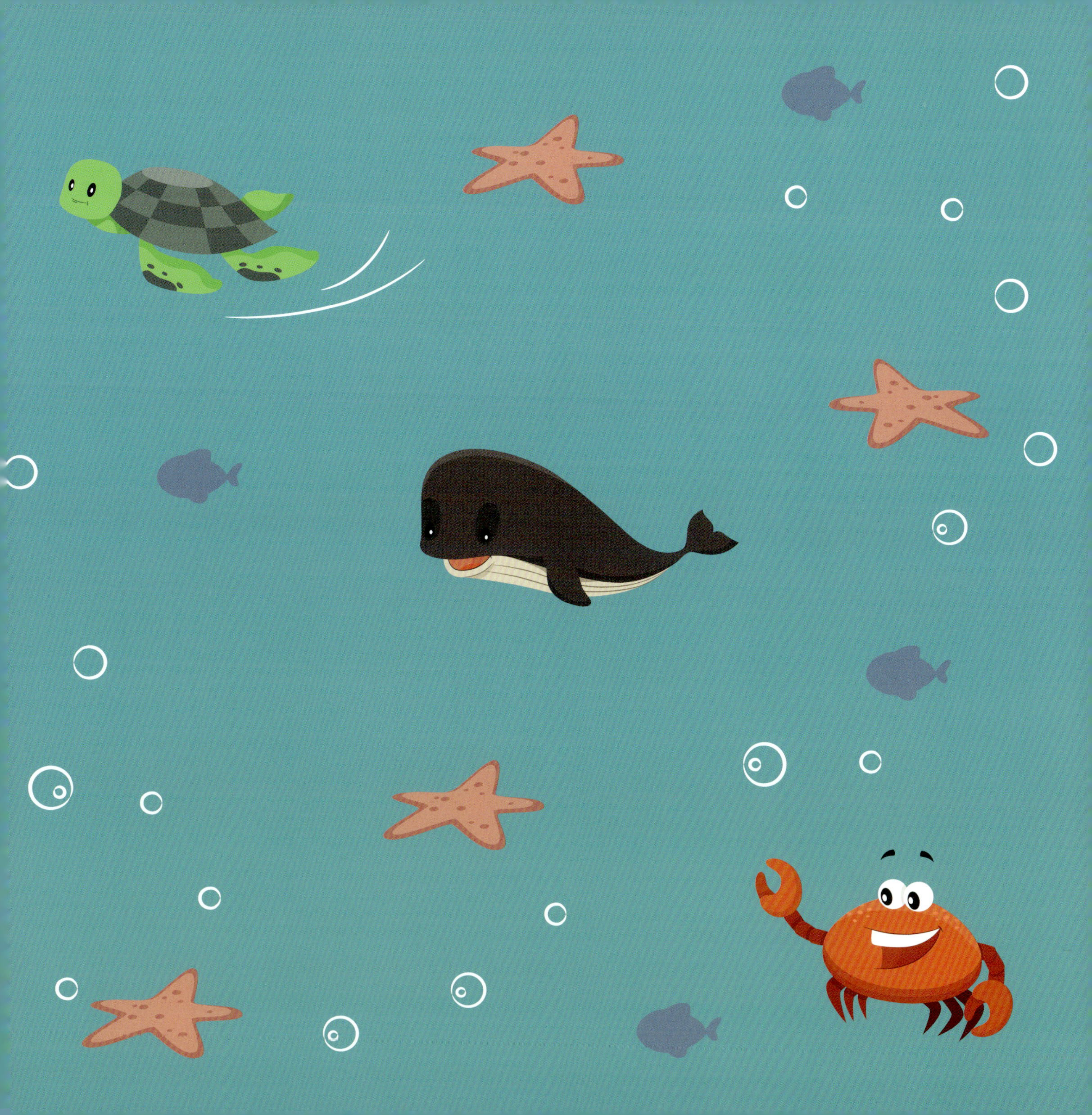

How many turtles can you count?

Can you lead Oscar to the reef?

1 2 3

Can you find the way through the maze?

Can you fill in the missing letters?

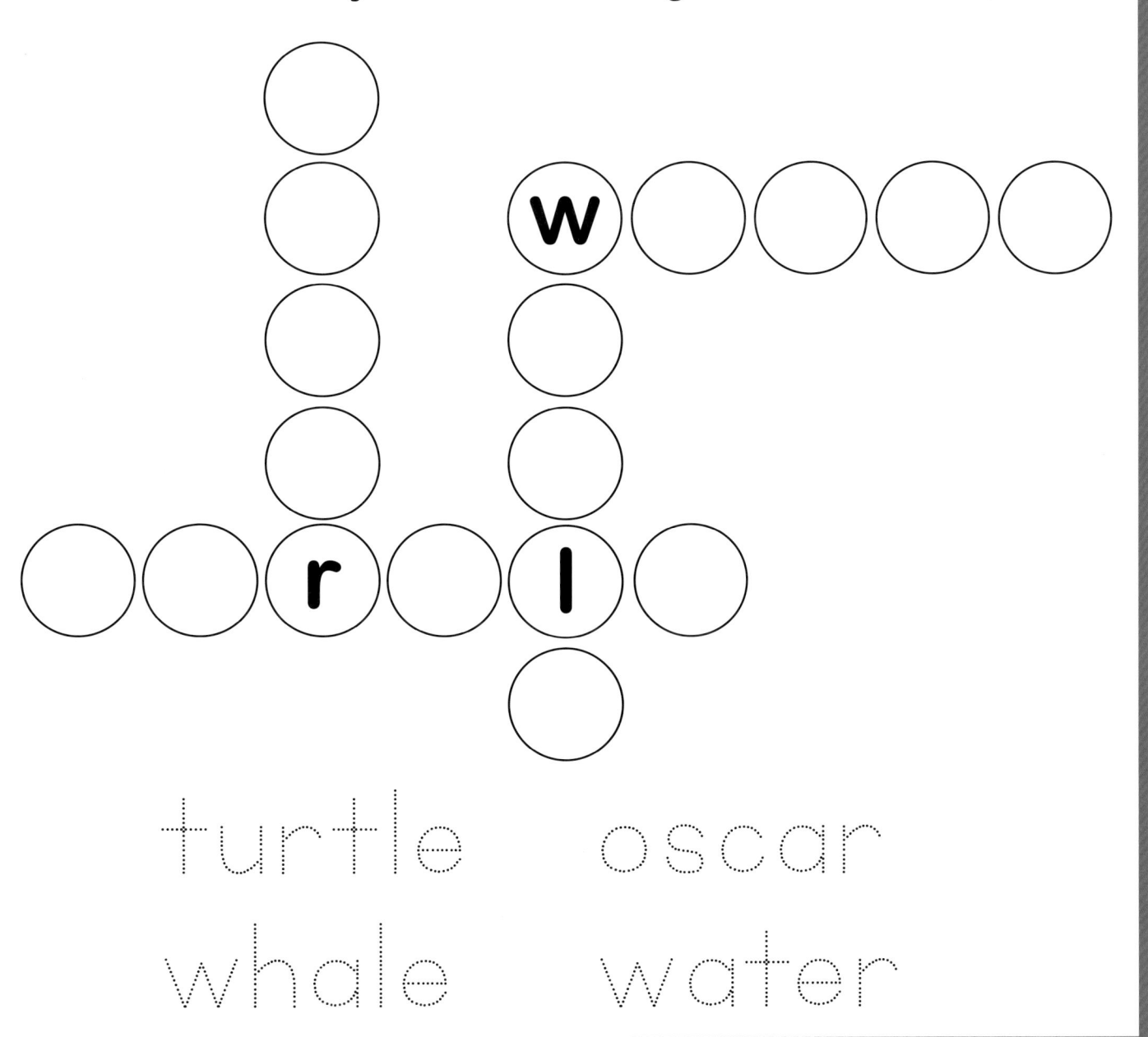

turtle   oscar

whale   water

OCEAN SERIES

www.messyentertainment.com

Search 'Messy Entertainment'
for books, apps & much more.